CW00859971

The Stress-Free Baby Names Book

How to Choose the Perfect Baby Name
with Confidence, Clarity and Calm

ASTON SANDERSON

"The Stress-Free Baby Names Book" by Aston Sanderson. Published by Walnut Publishing Company, Hanover Park, IL 60133

www.walnutpub.com

DEDICATION

To all new parents, and the exciting journey they're embarking on.

BONUS
FREE BOOK CLUB OFFER

Before we get started with this book, we just wanted to tell you about our Free Book Club email list.

Subscribe to the Free Book Club at **www.walnutpub.com** for more books from author Aston Sanderson, and free new releases from Walnut Publishing.

Thanks for buying, and enjoy reading.

CONTENTS

INTRODUCTION

"What's in a name? That which we call a rose by any other name would smell as sweet,"

— William Shakespeare

Congrats! I'm so happy and honored that you've chosen The Stress-Free Baby Names Book to help you find and choose the perfect name for your baby!

Becoming a parent is an important and amazing journey, whether you're becoming a parent for the first time, or once again. I'm so elated to be a small part of it.

HOW TO USE THIS BOOK

This book has two parts:

PART I: Chapters on naming.

Twelve written chapters with advice about how to select a baby name and what to consider during the process.

PART II: Baby Names List

A giant list of more than 3,000 girls', boys' and unisex names to inspire you, get you started, and maybe find the perfect name!

BONUS: Worksheets

Brainstorming worksheets to help you narrow down your choices and move forward with the process with your partner

The most important part of this book, however, is that you get the most of out of it. Think one of our chapters of advice is total codswallop? Don't like some of the names in our list? That's up to you, and feel free to ignore them!

But maybe you'll also find you really identify with one of the strategies I've broken down in one of our Naming Strategies chapters, or you just want to know how to deal with pressure from your family. This book can be digested as a whole, or taken in bits and pieces. It's whatever is most helpful to you to be happy with your baby name decision.

Ultimately, the choice is yours, for your family and child. It's not your mom's decision. Or your aunt's. Or the nosy neighbor's. Or your opinionated friend. Or even mine! It's 100% yours, and I hope I can help you find the perfect name for your baby!

PART I

CHAPTER 1
FINDING THE PERFECT NAME

OK, I know that in the last sentence you just read of the introduction of this book, I told you that this book would help you find the capital-P "Perfect" baby name! But guess what? It doesn't exist.

It's not out there, ready to be found by you, if only you can read thousands of name, sifting through them like hay looking for the needle. It's not a long-lost relative who will inspire you with the perfect classic-and-historical but also sounds-just-right-for-this-decade-and-cultural-moment-and-zeitgesit name. It's not going to be worth hundreds of hours of planning and thinking and considering. Trust me.

How do I know you won't find the perfect name? Because you will create it.

No, I don't mean you're going to make it up out of thin air. (But if you want to make up a new name that has never existed before, hey, you do you!)

You're going to make a perfect name because you're going to give it to your child, a human you've created (or adopted or any other way you've become a parent), a child you will raise and care for and love unconditionally and that is why it will be a perfect name.

Do you know how many parents freak out about naming their kid before it comes, and then once the child arrives, totally love the name? I hear from many people that they wish they had known how perfect a name would sound once they held that tiny person in their arms, even if it didn't feel perfect when they were choosing it.

Part of preparing for a child (especially your first) is over-preparing. Over-preparing can be caused by nervousness, a healthy dose or practicality, and

1

the pressures of the outside world.

We all want to be perfect parents, and having a kid is a huge, heck of a scary thing! You are responsible for another human being. One you've given life to.

Of course, preparing to be a parent is important. We should all be prepared, to a reasonable degree. But then there's also the tendency to give into our nervousness, the ancient, simple, reptile part of our brain that tells us we can fail or be bad parents or not do everything 100% perfect. One of the ways to stamp down this stress and fear is to obsess about details that aren't the most important. Like a name.

Listen here: You'll choose a wonderful name. You won't mess up your kid forever by choosing one that isn't capital-P Perfect. Their success doesn't depend on a gender-neutral name or a trendy name or a classic name. Their success depends on everything else: your love, you being present, you knowing when a small detail, a name, is not worth stressing over.

Choose a name you love. Or like well enough. Choose a name that fits and feels right. But if nothing feels all-important "Perfect," seriously, it's OK. You might not find the perfect name.

You can't find the perfect name, in essence. Because a name isn't perfect. You know what will be perfect? That name on your kid.

Now go forth, and let me help you spend a reasonable amount of time picking out a name, and not stressing out about it. It's time for the Stress-Free Baby Names guide to get to work for you! Sit back, relax, and let me do the hard stuff.

CHAPTER 2
MEANING AND ORIGIN

I'll dive in during the next chapter to different naming strategies, like whether to go unique, trendy, classic, super unique or semi-unique with your baby's name. But first, I'd like to make a point about meaning and origin.

For some parents, choosing a name based on the linguistic origin of the name and meaning are important. But for most of us, I'd argue that it really doesn't matter that much.

Sure, maybe you want your daughter's name to mean "beauty," or your son's name to mean "strength." Or the other way around. But outside of one school project in 2nd grade, how often will the linguistic meaning or origin of your child's name come up? It doesn't really make a difference. What will matter most over the course of a lifetime is the name itself.

Now, a note here: This is not to say that you can't choose a name that has an important meaning or origin to you, like a family origin or association meaning (to a friend, beloved book character, etc.).

I'm just saying that basing your child's name on an origin or meaning that has no connection to you, like the types of meaning and origins you see in, yes, baby name books, is a bit silly. That meaning often will not come up in conversation, ever, unless you force it.

Why choose a name for this reason when you could instead think about all the other reasons and factors that will have an actual impact on your child's life? For instance, how the name will position your child in their generation, how it will sound with their middle and last name, how it will go with your and your partner's name and any siblings, or what sort of pop culture or well-known associations the name has in people's minds?

Those reasons are a bit more important for most people's purposes, and that's what we'll cover in this book. We included in this book a list of more than 3,000 baby names to get you started in your search. And we haven't included meanings or origins, and this is why: We think you should focus on other aspects that matter more.

Listen, if linguistic meanings and origins are your thing, definitely go for it! We still have some great advice in this book we think you'd like to read. And our list can be a starting place for you to find new names or remember old ones you'd forgotten about but still love.

Now, let's dive in to the good stuff and find your little bundle the perfect name — and save you the worry and stress of this process— to make it as easy and smooth as possible! Just read our chapters, use our worksheets, and in no time you will have the perfect name for your little one!

CHAPTER 3
NAMING STRATEGIES: FROM CLASSIC TO TRENDY TO TOTALLY UNIQUE

In this chapter, we will go through many different naming strategies for your kid. This will be the longest chapter in the book, and the one you may find most useful.

BENEFITS OF A CLASSIC NAME

First things first: You really can't go wrong with a classic name. For example, classic names for boys are: William, John, James, Joseph. Or for girls: Elizabeth, Catherine, Emma, Lillian. They are classic, common, timeless. People will always know how to pronounce them (in large English-speaking countries at least, but maybe your little one will grow up to be a world traveler, of course!)

The benefits to this naming strategy are that your kid's name won't be jarring or surprising to people. Kids with unique names have to deal with constant mispronunciation, misspelling, misunderstanding, and comments on their "interesting" name their entire lives.

If your kid has a classic name, they won't have to face any of those problems.

These names also sound classic, so usually pair quite well with any last name.

Another good strategy is to use a classic name as a middle name. This gives your kid an insurance policy. If they end up really not liking their first name for whatever reason, (let's say they end up sharing it with an embarrassing young starlet, like if you named your kid Paris about 15 years ago...) they have a classic, sure-fire normal name to use instead. It's quite common for people to go by their middle name, and it is still a legal name so can prevent any problems that just choosing random names out out of the blue might cause.

DOWNSIDES TO A CLASSIC NAME

So what are the downsides to going with a classic or timeless name? Well, it will be shared with a lot of other classmates and people. Common names can mean trouble for email addresses, mail mix-ups, identity mix-ups, or sharing a name with someone online who happens to have a criminal record.

But usually, these names can be so common as to be totally fine for those sorts of things. There will be so many people with the same name, the name almost can't become anything bad or negatively associated with it.

What's the flipside of "normal," or "common," though? The flipside is "boring." This may not be an issue for some people. One man's boring is another man's classic, and that's great. It's up to you! Let's move on to the next naming strategy now that I've covered classic names.

ON TRENDY NAMES

Alright, parents, let's get to the bottom of it: A lot of the names you probably think are unique right now are actually the most popular names of the moment. They appear to be unique because they are so different and differently-sounding than the classic names we discussed in the last chapter. You've heard them a few times, but not very often. Something about it just sounds perfect but you're not sure why. Well, it's probably because the name is at the top of the current trending list.

In 2015 (the most recent year US government data was available), the top boy's names were:
1.   Noah
2.   Liam
3.   Mason
4.   Jacob
5.   William

The top girl's names in 2015 were:
1.   Emma
2.   Olivia
3.   Sophia
4.   Ava
5.   Isabella

It is easy to miss what names are trending at the moment. It's hard to know everyone is naming their kids that because your baby is on the way, not just getting signed up for preschool and meeting the other seven "Noahs" in the class. Especially if you're not surrounded by friends having children, you may be out of the loop of what other parents are going with.

But, these trendy names are one way to go. Like the classic names, they will not be mispronounced, misspelled, misunderstood, or uncommon, at least for your kid's generation. Just like the most popular names in 1920 for girls were Mary, Dorothy, Helen, Margaret, and Ruth, those names now sound like elderly women names, because they were popular for that generation.

So you can feel safe that your kid can enjoy all the benefits of having a classic name, while also having a name that ties them specifically to their generation. For instance, when your kid is young, they will have a kid-sounding name. When they are 40-something, they will have a middle-aged-sounding name. And when they are a senior citizen, they will have an old-sounding name. So your kid will get to age with their generation.

Trendy names could be a great naming strategy! Just that word of caution I mentioned at the beginning of this section: The names you think are semi-unique may actually be really popular at the moment! But that doesn't mean they aren't great names. Just check the recent years' baby names lists to see how your top names compare.

But what if you do want a semi-unique name? Read more in the section below:

ON SEMI-UNIQUE NAMES

But what about a name that is semi-unique? Not way out there, but not trendy, and not classic? These might be the names you'd find at the bottom of the top 100 most popular names lists. These names may provoke a little misunderstanding, but they will be unique to your child, especially more so than trendy names, or the names at the top of the recent years' most popular lists.

It is a little safer than going for a really unique name, but a little more unique than just going for straight trendy or classic names.

But remember — you never know what will happen in the future. A name that is unique now is not guaranteed to safely stay unique over time (especially once your little pumpkin has it and is an all-around amazing human and a ton of other parents and community members want to copy you until the name is famous. OK, that may happen, but maybe it will not).

Regardless, you can't predict the future. Maybe the name that is unique now will be at the top of popular baby name lists in 10 years, or 20. There's just no way to know. But do you research, and check out the resources I've provided for you to do some research into whether that unique name you've chosen is really unique. Let's move on to the last naming strategy.

GOING TOTALLY UNIQUE

Alright, so you want to go totally out there? Like famous celebrity baby names "Apple" (daughter of Coldplay front-man Chris Martin and actress Gwyneth Paltrow) and "Moon Unit?" (daughter of Frank Zappa)?

If celebrities can do it, why not you? Indeed. If you are ready to go super unique, go for it! Live your truth, do what makes you happy in your heart. But first — a few considerations.

ARE YOU ACTUALLY READY FOR AN OUT-THERE NAME?

First: a note on spelling. If you are going to go for a unique name, just having a unique spelling of a regular name (Jesika, Cyndee, Mykel) will actually not be unique — as your child's name will actually just be pronounced like Jessica, Cindy or Michael. And it will cause a lifetime of headaches for your son or daughter, especially when it comes to government forms, calling any customer support help line, or just getting through life with a common name pronounced commonly but spelled in quite an uncommon way.

Then it also has the effect in the opposite direction: Whenever people try to pronounce the name, they'll assume it surely can't be pronounced like the common name, otherwise, why is it spelled that way?

Sure, I understand, having a unique name is not about pleasing the masses. But remember that a name, ultimately, is about communication. It's what everyone will use to call your son or daughter from the time they are born to the time they are 90+ years old. It will be the word with the most neural connections in their brain, and the way they will most frequently interact with the world, whether they intend to or not. So making that name something that hinders communication, confuses it, or breaks it down unnecessarily, will cause some headaches and annoyance for your kid. We all know these people with unusual names, and if we know them well enough, we know how annoyed they can be. (If we don't know them well enough, we still may not even be sure how to pronounce their name or spell it!)

Are you ready to defend it to family members, strangers, and others? Depending on how unique the name is, plan for some pushback from people. Usually people are pretty good about respecting the name a parent has chosen, but be prepared for people to try to question you about it, even in a polite way.

DO YOUR RESEARCH ON A UNIQUE NAME

Make sure to Google the name and/or word you've chosen, just to see what associations are already out there with it. You never know what weird company has been using the name in relative obscurity for years but will cause it to unwittingly come up in any Google search anyone performs on your kid. So just make sure to do a check before signing the name away on the birth certificate.

There is always the possibility that the name will not be liked by your child as they get older. So one tactic to take is to give them a unique first name (or middle name) and then do a common first name or middle name, so they can choose to swap to the other if it really doesn't fit them well.

Some names, also, that are very unique may sound strange at first to people, but if your kid grows into the name and has a personality to match, people will think your kid is especially awesome and probably be jealous that they couldn't pull off a name with so much spunk like your kid with the huge personality. What if they turn out to be a wallflower and are embarrassed by the name though? These are the things to consider.

Another thing to think about is the hiring process, as boring as that sounds. Will a super unique name hurt your kid's chances of getting callbacks for job interviews, or will it make them stand out more? Imagine you are hiring for a company, and imagine a resume with the name you are thinking of giving your kid that is unique. Does it still sound professional?

BENEFITS OF A UNIQUE NAME

But what will be the benefits? Your kid will stand out with a unique name. And the 15 Jacobs in his kindergarten class might be jealous that he gets to be just Frad instead of Jacob W or blond Jacob or however they decide to demarcate all the un-unique, boring kid names in class.

It will probably be easier for your kid to get their username on websites, acquire a Gmail address, and do personal branding if they want to open up their own business later in life (or be an author, like your favorite author Aston Sanderson right here…).

Also be aware that more parents are going outside the norm these days, so you will be in good company by going a little out there. In the old days, practically everyone named their kid classic names. Now, people get more creative and feel more comfortable going outside the norm. So, yes, even when trying to be unique these days, you still may be following trends by being unique. It's a bit tiresome to try to wrap your brain around, huh?

So, ultimately, my best advice is to just go unusual if you want! Just be aware of common pitfalls for parents trying to go unique, and do your best to do your research.

Now that you know all about the different naming strategies — whether you want to go classic, unique, semi-unique or trendy — I can move on to just how you'll go about choosing that name. Time to learn more about naming your special little one! In the next few chapters, I'll talk about pronunciation, nicknames, and other considerations..

CHAPTER 4
CHOOSING ADVICE

"Nicknames stick to people, and the most ridiculous are the most adhesive,"

— Thomas Chandler Haliburton

"i love nicknames. It makes me feel loved. It makes me feel less alone in this world,"

— Ellen Page

Onto some advice on how to choose that precious little one's name. So far I've talked about different strategies you can take in naming your child. You can go common or classic, trendy at the moment or a little unique, or totally out-there unique and special.

Whichever way you go is up to you, but no matter which method you take, these next three chapters on choosing advice will apply and help walk you through the steps to making sure you avoid the common pitfalls and choose the most perfect name possible for your special little kid. Let's get to it:

SOUND IT OUT

A very important part of your kid's name is the way it sounds. The name won't just be written, but said millions of times over the course of your child's full life.

So make sure to say it aloud. Let it roll off your tongue. Say it sweetly and softly. Yell it happily like you're cheering your kid on across the soccer field. Yell it angrily like Jr. has just run away from you in the supermarket. (We all pretend we're never going to yell, not once, before we become parents, but please tell me of one person you know who has actually followed their belief in this).

SOUNDS & HOW THEY ARE PERCEIVED

Believe it or not, there are a lot of subtle sound associations with different letters, sounds, vowels, consonants and letter groupings that we hear on a daily basis. This is especially pertinent in advertising, where you want the name of a car to sound strong and slick (like Porsche) while others sound…well, a bit weak and strange. (like the Wingle: Yes, an actual name from a Chinese car manufacturer for a car model.)

The same applies to names for people. The name Xena is going to sound stronger than Daisy, at least with pop culture associations, but how does the name actually sound in terms of the letters?

Names that sound breathier, or have fewer hard consonants, may sound a bit less forceful. Like Hannah (soft) vs. Jackie (hard), or Charles (soft) vs. Eric (hard).

CONSIDER THE FULL NAME

When sounding out your kid's name, it will be especially important to combine it with any middle name you choose to give him or her as well as your last name. Beware of tongue-twister first-middle-last name combinations!

Also be especially aware of rhyming and the repetition of certain sounds. My own name veers into that territory: Aston Sanderson has two "As" sounds in it. Two is enough; if my middle name had this sound as well, it would be a bit much. For example:

Aston Michael Sanderson (ok) (and my actual real name)
vs.
Aston Samson Sanderson (too much sound repetition)

So make sure all the names flow together and sound good. You want them to roll off the tongue and be a beautiful combination of sounds and names.

WHAT ABOUT SIBLINGS?

Another thing to think about along with your child's full name is how it works within the family unit. Do you already have other kids, or plan on having more? How do all the first names of your children sound together? How does the new child's name sound with your first name, or your partner's? For example, you may sign your family Christmas cards as "The Hendersons," but you may also sign it with all of your first names, so make sure the collection of those names sounds good.

I also have one word of caution if you want to name your children something similar to their siblings: Naming your daughters Leah and Leslie will mean a lifetime of them being confused for each other and called each other's names by elderly relatives and family friends.

INITIALS

Also look at initials: Don't name your kid Aaron Sean Smith, for example, or Dorothy Ursa Mitchell. You don't want to open your kid to a lifetime of teasing with embarrassing initials, and I'll look more at avoiding nicknames and the cruelty of children in the next chapter.

ASSOCIATIONS FROM THE OUTSIDE WORLD

Kids can be cruel. That is the crux of these next few sections, which are about nicknames and other associations for the name you are going to choose for your child.

If you name your kid Lola, for example, or Cecilia, they might forever be cursed with people singing to them the moment they meet them. Or if you name your kid Beyoncé, well, that's certainly an association that will follow them around their entire life. It may seem cute now, but that is a name the kid will have to live with forever.

What other associations will your child's name stir? If your last name is Potter, and you want to use Henry because it is a family name dating back generations, it will still be more associated with Harry Potter than with your dad, grandpa and great-uncle all named Henry Potter. Think about the associations the outside world might force upon your innocent little kid.

NICKNAMES

As I have mentioned, kids can be cruel. So your kid might end up with an unfortunate nickname from classmates that you didn't intend. Think:

What does the name rhyme with?
What does it sound like with your last name?
If you shorten the name, what does it rhyme with?
If you shorten your last name, what does it rhyme with?
Remember again about initials — what do they spell?

And if you love a full name, like Elizabeth, but can't stand Liz, Eliza, Beth or any other shortening, remember that you can't control what your kid will end up preferring as they grow up. Maybe your daughter really feels like a Beth in her heart of hearts, even if you really see her as an Elizabeth.

And friends especially will shorten names, even if it is against your daughter's wishes as well, maybe her friends just really want to call her "E" all the time. So you won't be able to choose what your kid is called, and must be ready and prepared for all variations of the birth name you choose and accept them all into your life.

You may think that you get license to always call your son or daughter whatever you want throughout their life anyway, but remember, they may decide one day that they really prefer to be called something else, so always remember that you need to be flexible no matter what.

ASSOCIATIONS FROM THE "INSIDE" WORLD

During the choosing process, a lot of old name associations start to rise up for many of us that we didn't remember we even had.

Maybe you really love the name Amber but it is the name of a character you really hate on a TV show, or it's your partner's ex, or it's the annoying cube-mate of your friend at work, or it's the dog walker, or it's the inefficient bag person at the grocery store, or any number of small acquaintances you run into throughout the course of your lived life.

But what if you really like the name and your partner has a small bad association? Or you really like the name, but just remembered, oh yeah, that was the name of the bully in my school growing up?

I've got great news for you if this is the case: All those small associations will fall away once you give this name to your child. Think about it: You haven't met your child yet, and they are still just a blank slate, a person you can't yet imagine or hold or see living in the world. All you have to go on is blurry ultrasounds and what you imagine will happen in the future and how you currently feel.

But soon that little ultrasound picture will be a living, breathing, fully-formed human, and he or she will become your everything. And all other associations will fall away. It will no longer be the dog walker or the person who hit your car three months ago. It will just be your daughter or son, and all the other associations won't matter, because you will have a real person to stand in for those associations, and they will be your favorite person in the world. That awesome new member of your family will grow into that name more and more every day.

YOUR BABY WILL BE A FULL-FLEDGED ADULT SOME DAY

So a lot of the planning of preparing for a baby surrounds pregnancy, the moments leading up to birth, the birthing process, and the immediacy after birth. You probably don't spend a ton of time sitting around imagining your little peanut-to-be working at a corporate office and wearing a tie at 45.

But that may be their life someday! Whether your baby grows up to be a lawyer, an astronaut, a circus performer, a writer, a truck driver or a manager, they will grow up, that's for sure.

So you need to make sure the name you choose is not just appropriate for an infant, baby and toddler in cute little outfits, but for a teenager, for a 20-something fresh out of college and ready to hit the job market, for a middle-aged person, for a father or a mother themselves and finally, for an aging senior citizen.

Thinking of an appropriate name for a senior citizen may be, I admit, thinking a bit too far ahead. So let's stop at that stage right after teenager: A 20-something out of college and hitting the job market.

Is the name professional enough for your kid if they decide to be a corporate lawyer, or does it sound only appropriate for an avant-garde artist? You never know what the future holds for the life of your little one, so make sure to let the world be as big as their dreams, and allow them to have any opportunities they want.

Don't accidentally hinder them with their name. Make sure it is one that can allow them to be anything and achieve anything they want. Of course, a name won't actually stop someone who is very determined from achieving their dreams. But that's not what this book is about, OK? It's about names, so do your best to give the future life of your child at least a few thoughts before choosing an uber-cute-for-a-baby name. They'll thank you for it, trust me.

A helpful thought exercise to help you imagine your baby-to-be as a grown-up person is to think of what you would want to be named were you to start your life over. What name would give you the most advantages, sound super cool, and set you up for success, as much as a name is able to? What name would you adopt, right now?

YOU DON'T NEED TO EXPRESS YOURSELF

While you are pregnant, there is a lot of pressure. People always, always want to talk about the baby, about being pregnant, what is your birth plan, have you thought of any names yet? It can be a lot of pressure to put on a new mom or dad.

Sometimes the whirlwind of being pregnant can overshadow the little life that's about to start. Of course, being pregnant is all about preparing for the little life that is about to be born. But there is a lot of crazy hoopla that surrounds pregnancy: A ton of unsolicited advice from acquaintances and strangers, endless showers, parties and gifts, worry and preparation for the first few weeks, for the birthing process, telling family and making them a part of the process and of course: Figuring out a name! It's a lot to take in. (But don't stress. This guide is here to help you choose a baby name-stress-free, so that's at least one thing to cross of the huge to-do list.)

People will want to be impressed by you and everything that you have come up with for your newborn. You may feel stressed out trying to impress people with how creative you are with the name. People will immediately judge your baby's name, and you must get over that.

It doesn't need to say anything about you, your personality, your creativity, or your life. It doesn't need to say anything about your child, either. It is just a name.

And you are choosing the name that is best for your little one; so don't feel held up worrying about how it will reflect on you, no matter how much other people want to talk all about it.

CHAPTER 5
HOW TO DEAL WITH FAMILY AND OUTSIDE PRESSURE

There is a lot of outside pressure, oftentimes, when are having a baby and choosing a name. You can feel outside pressure from your family, your friends, your partner or tradition.

That can be a lot to deal with! But remember the No. 1 Golden Rule: This is about your baby, not your friends, your church, your parents, or what anyone else says. Like we went over in the last chapter, the name you choose should be the one that you think feels right.

FAMILY NAMES

If you are open to naming your child in the family tradition, or want to harken back to a relative, immediate or distant, with your name, you can do so, and choosing this naming route is often a nice way to honor family (or friends, as, as we all know, friends can become as close as if not closer than family).

You can choose the actual name of a distant relative for your child, just adopting the name straight, as it is, or you can do a creative twist on a family name. For example, is there a tradition of men in your family being named William? Name your son Liam, which means "son of William." Then you have a new twist on the name, without having to use the name itself. Another example: Your partner's grandmother is Ann and your grandma is Mary? How about Anna Marie?

There are many different creative ways to honor a loved one without being tied to using that person's exact name. You can put a twist on the name and find one that works best for you and that feels new and fresh even if it is an older name.

FAMILY PRESSURE

However, if you have pressure from your family to choose a family name, and you really don't want to, remember an important point about naming your child. Remember in the first chapter about choosing the perfect name (Why You Can't Find the "Perfect" Name — But You Will Anyway)? We talked about how even if a name doesn't feel perfect before the birth, it will begin to suit your child and you will love it more and more each day.

It should be the same for your family. Even if their initial reaction to the name is not overwhelmingly positive, they will slowly over time realize that the name is for the child that they love, and it will grow on them, too. So what works for you will also work for your family.

PRESSURE FROM FRIENDS & OTHER OUTSIDE INFLUENCES

Are your friends pressuring you to choose a regular name? Are you feeling like your culture, community or small group of parents in the neighborhood will judge you? I'm here to say: Forget them.

Name your child what you want. Family pressure is one thing, but strangers? Who cares what they think? Friends may be a bit different. But still — what kind of friends are they if they are pressuring you about your child's name?

As for other outside pressure in the neighborhood, of course, you must also think about how your child will grow up in his or her community. Will the name be reason for teasing? That's never good. But also, learning to be strong in the face of being different is what "The Ugly Duckling" fairytale is all about, right?

All in all, don't worry too much about outside pressure. Do what makes you and your partner and your future child happy! That is what truly matters.

DECIDE WHAT'S IMPORTANT

Ultimately, it's up to you how much you want to bend to outside pressure. Maybe you want to go rogue and do whatever you want, even if it displeases your family. But if pleasing your family or fitting into societal norms makes you happy, then by all means, do that! The choice is yours, and my book is here to tell you that whatever choice you want to make is the right one.

CHAPTER 6
COMMUNICATION WITH YOUR PARTNER

Deciding on a name for your baby should be a couple's decision. Even if your partner says, "I don't care, choose whatever name you want," it is good to clue them into your naming process. Like over-obsessing about naming your child as a way to combat the stress of becoming a new parent, trying to totally stay out of the process can be another way to attempt to deal with that stress.

You both made the kid, did you not? (Or went through the adoption process together, or any other non-traditional means of becoming parents). So you can both decide on the name, or at least have a say.

Here are some basic rules for communication with your partner that you may find helpful in all areas of life, and not just during the time you are deciding on a name during pregnancy:

BE OPEN AND HONEST

As in most forms of communication, more is better. Be open with your partner about the names you like, and why you like them.

If your partner immediately dismisses a name, find out why. But you also must be willing to share the "why" with your partner as well if you immediately don't like a name, even if you feel embarrassed about the reason (a short fling in college? The name of the guy whose car you wrecked in high school in that accident?)

Also identify what is important to you in naming your child. Share your values with your partner. Is it important to honor family? Is it important to choose a trendy name? Is it important the name starts with the same letter as your mom's name? Communicate what you are thinking and what is important to you.

BE A GOOD LISTENER & NONJUDGMENTAL

On the flip side of being open and honest, you also must be willing to hear what your partner is saying.

What is important to your partner in a name may not be important to you; or it may sound trivial. But you also should be nonjudgmental. What is important to you is very subjective, just like what is important to your partner. You may have different ways of approaching how important names are, what they should stand for, and how to ultimately choose one.

That's OK! Because if you have open communication, you may disagree on a few things when it comes to the naming process, but that is when we get to:

COMPROMISE

If you love love love a name, but your partner detests it, it's probably not going to work out. It's better to find a name you both love 80% than one of you feel 100% great about and your partner feels 0% great about.

You may feel disappointed when you tell your partner the name you love and they don't like it all. Sure, they may come around in time, but there's also a huge possibility they will not be able to get over their initial reaction.

So be prepared to let some "perfect" names go, and don't fall into the trap of believing they seem more "perfect" because you can't have them.

I have added some worksheets at the end of this book for your partner and you to work together on choosing a name, if you'd like the added help of a guided way to talk about the names that are important to you and figure out your values.

CHAPTER 7
TO TELL — OR NOT TO TELL?

When you've decided on a name, you'll probably feel super excited, as you should! That's going to be the name of your child! You may be tempted to shout it from the rooftops and email every one you've ever met and post it on Facebook and tell strangers in the street.

Most people, however, recommend keeping the name for your child — even if it's just a hard "maybe" at this point — to yourself. Everyone and their mom will have a huge opinion on the baby name you have chosen, and they may not all be favorable. People will draw from all areas of their life to explain to you why they don't like it. No name is going to get a 100% positive response.

If you keep the name to yourself until you have your son or daughter, people may complain behind your back about the name, but they should have the decency not to do it to your face, so who cares what they think then! They will pretend to love it, and that will save you all the grief of getting their honest opinions while pregnant.

While you (or your partner) is pregnant, people will see the name as not yet "set" in stone. So they may assume you are asking for a critique or a reason to change your mind. Once the child has been officially named, they don't see that name as flexible anymore, and so will not give you as much of a critique.

There is one bonus to sharing the name, and that is feedback. Maybe your friends or family or even a stranger will think of something you didn't realize about the name. Something it rhymes with, some famous embarrassing celebrity it reminds them of, or something else you didn't think of.

But there's a way to get feedback without suffering the judgment of family and friends: Do it anonymously on an online forum. If you need to sign up to one, find a free one and share your chosen baby name anonymously. Strangers will tell you their honest opinion, and maybe you will gather some good information. Maybe they assume it is a girl's name when it is a boy's or the other way around, or maybe they don't know how to pronounce it. But ultimately, they are strangers on the internet, so you have the freedom to ignore them in a way you wouldn't be able to ignore your friends and family. Thank goodness!

Strangers online will also have less of an emotional reaction, as they do not know you, and cannot imagine the future little person in their life, so they will not be as emotionally and intensely reacting, also saving you some headaches were you to reveal it to people you knew in person. You have control how much you will bow to outside pressure.

CHAPTER 8
RESOURCES: WEBSITES FOR RESEARCH

In a few of these chapters, I mentioned doing some research before going with a name for your child. These two resources will help you to gain a little more context around the popularity over time of the name you want to choose, or can show you which names have been popular in the US.

SOCIAL SECURITY GOVERNMENT WEBSITE

On the Social Security Administrations' government website, you can find data on the most popular baby names in a few different ways.

You can find out the most popular baby names by decade (all the way back from the 1880s until 2010), popular names by state, statistics on popularity change over time, the top 5 names, year by year, over the last 100 years, and the top names, overall, over the last 100 years.

Start browsing this website by following the link here:
http://bit.ly/ssababynames

BABY NAME WIZARD

This website has so much fascinating data, you could get lost for hours. If you just want to skim the surface, however, (remember, make the process stress-free! Sometimes more information is too much information and paralyzing instead of helpful), you can use this tool to search the top names you are considering for your baby to see how their popularity has changed over the last 135 years.

Just plug the name into where it says "Name Voyager" (not where it says

"Search for a Name" in orange at the top) to see a chart showing the rise and fall of that name over years.

Putting in the name "Elisa," for example, shows that it remained a relatively uncommon name until it exploded in 1960s to 1980s. It then saw an unprecedented, huge spike in popularity around 2011, but swiftly dropped off.

You can also double click on the chart to go to a page containing name facts (like linguistic origin). One of the most helpful features on this page is where you can find "Related Names." For "Elisa," a few related names are "Elise, Eliza, Alisa, Lisa." This is a phenomenal way to find names similar to ones you like, and maybe discover a new one you hadn't thought of.

You can browse the Baby Name Voyager by following the link here:
http://bit.ly/babyvoyager

CHAPTER 9
CONCLUSION

We have gone through the different naming strategies you can take (timeless and classic, trendy or semi-unique, and very unique), given you some choosing advice (be open with your partner, sound it out, think of middle and last name and siblings, think of your child being an adult, consider nicknames and the cruelty of kids, think of cultural associations and famous people) and hopefully helped you get on your way to choosing the perfect baby name for your new son or daughter!

The most important takeaway from this book should be that you shouldn't stress or spend a ton of time on picking a name, you should only spend however much time it takes to consider each of the points I've raised in this book, and you've had a good, hashed-out discussion with your partner, and the name feels mostly right.

Because even if it doesn't feel perfect, there could be any number of factors why it doesn't feel perfect, and they could be that you are feeling nervous about properly raising a little person to be a wonderful, thoughtful, smart, talented, kind, interesting and loving human in this messy, complicated and harsh world of ours.

Once your son or daughter is born, all will be right. You will not be able to imagine him or her ever having any other name. It will be the Perfect baby name. Yes, with a capital P. Many new parents say this: That they wish they had known how little the name would matter, and also how much it would matter once it was attached to their child.

I also recommend that you don't put off this decision. There's a lot of paperwork you have to do before leaving the hospital, so don't delay getting home and getting started with your new life with your little one. It's best to choose before going into labor. There's enough to think about during the birthing process.

Some people think that they will know which name feels right upon seeing their child's face for the first time, but oftentimes, this just leads to feeling even more pressure about the name, especially when you don't have a name to announce to friends and family eagerly awaiting the birth.

Let's get real: Most babies just look like babies. You won't be able to distinguish whether your baby looks like a "John," "Jacob" or "James." So decide on that name before entering the hospital.

In the next few chapters, I have some resources to help you choose the best baby name. Chapter 14 covers websites for further research, Chapter 15 includes baby naming worksheets if you feel stuck or just need some help, and Chapter 16 has our list of more than 3,000 baby names for girls, boys and unisex names. These resources are not the end-all-be-all, but hopefully they will help you in your journey.

THANKS FOR READING

Thanks for reading "The Stress-Free Baby Names Book." I hope I was able to help you choose the perfect baby name with confidence, clarity and calm, as promised! I hope I at least helped you on your way and gave you some good strategies to think about as you embark on this important, life-changing journey we call becoming a parent.

We like to get real reader feedback, and would love to hear if you enjoyed the book, found it useful, or have suggestions for improvement. Please leave us a review on Amazon. You can leave a review by entering this URL in your browser: bit.ly/babynamesreview

PART II

THE BIG LIST OF BABY NAMES

In this section, you'll find 3,000 baby names, divided into sections for girls' names, boys' names and unisex names, or those that can be used for either sex.

BABY NAMES FOR GIRLS

A (Girls)

Aaliyah

Aaryen

Aba

Abayomi

Abebi

Abegaila

Abegail

Abelia

Abena

Abbey

Abha

Abiah

Abida

Abigail

Abiona

Abira

Abisha

Abra

Acacia

Acadia

Acantha

Aceline

Achala

Adah

Adalheidis

Adalia

Adalina

Adamma

Adanna

Adarra

Adelaide

Adeliza

Adelpha

Adelyne

Aderes

Adia

Adila

Adina

Adva

Aolha

Aonia

Adora

Adria

Adriane

Adya

Adyessa

Aegina

Aenea

Aeola

Aethra

Afiela

Afiya

Africa

Afra

Aryea

Agalia

Agatha

Aglaia

Agnes

Ahava	Akako	Alda
Ahia	Akamai	Aldarra
Ahilya	Akanesi	Aladea
Ahyoka	Akela	Aldreda
Ahyoko	Akhila	Alea
Ai	Aki	Aleen
Aida	Akilah	Alei
Aidan	Akilina	Alesa
Aideen	Akiva	Aleta
Aiko	Ala	Alethea
Aila	Alaia	Alexandra
Ailane	Alaine	Aley
Ailine	Alamea	Ali
Ailsa	Alana	Alice
Ain	Alani	Alicia
Aina	Alarice	Alile
Aine	Alauda	Alina
Ainsley	Alaudia	Alisa
Aisha	Alberta	Alisson
Aiyana	Albina	Alita
Ajeya	Alcina	Aliya
Akahana		Aliza

Altrinna	Amalthea	Ana
Alya	Amana	Anadaria
Alyriane	Amanda	Anais
Alma	Amara	Anala
Almena	Amaris	Ananda
Almera	Amaryllis	Anadita
Almodine	Amaya	Anastasia
Aloha	Amber	Anci
Alohani	Amberlynne	Andela
Alona	Amee	Andrea
Alonsa	Ameila	Andromeda
Alpha	America	Anea
Althaea	Amethyst	Anela
Aluna	Amicah	Anemone
Alva	Amiela	Angee
Alya	Amina	Angela
Alzena	Amira	Ani
Amabel	Amity	Aniani
Amadea	Amma	Anila
Amadi	Amor	Anina
Amala	Amy	Anisah
	Amymone	Ann

Annabelle	Ardah	Ashanti
Annamae	Ardelle	Ashley
Annamarie	Arden	Ashni
Annadora	Arella	Asia
Annora	Argenta	Asiza
Ansonia	Argentina	Asmee
Anthea	Aria	Aspen
Antoinette	Ariana	Asteria
Anwen	Arielle	Asya
Anya	Ariza	Atlanta
Aolani	Arlene	Athena
Aonani	Arlette	Atifa
Apangela	Armina	Atrina
Aphra	Arnina	Aubrey
Aphrodite	Artemis	Audrey
April	Artha	Aura
Aquene	Arvinda	Aurelia
Ara	Arwan	Aurora
Arabella	Asela	Autumn
Arabelle	Asenath	Ava
Arcadia	Asha	Aveline
Arcelia		Averleia

Avery

Avis

Avitalia

Awendela

Ayah

Ayalah

Ayanna

Ayasha

Ayda

Ayesha

Ayla

Ayodele

Ayoka

Ayondela

Ayumi

Azalea

Azami

Azaria

Aziza

Azriela

Azura

Azza

B (Girls)

Bathia

Bathilda

Bahira

Bambi

Bambina

Barbara

Beatrice

Belen

Belle

Benita

Berdine

Bernice

Bertille

Bethany

Bianca

Blaine

Blaire

Blessing

Blythe

Branca

Bree

Brenda

Brice

Bridge

Britanny

Brunelle

Bryn

C (Girls)

Cailin

Caitlin

Calantha

Candace

Candra

Carey

Carina

Carla

Carol

Caroline

Cassidy

Catherine

Cecilia

Celeste

Cerella

Cerise

Chameli

Chandelle

Chanel

Channa

Chantal

Chara

Charity

Charla

Charmaine

Chasia

Chasida

Chelsea

Cher

Cheyenne

Chiara

China

Chislaine

Chloe

Chloris

Christine

Ciara

Clara

Clementine

Colette

Colleen

Constance

Corey

Cornelia

Courtney

Cozette

Crystla

Cybelle

Cunthia

Cyrene

Cyrilla

Czarina

D (Girls)

Dacey

Dahlia

Damaris

Dana

Danaen

Daniah

Danica

Danielle

Daphne

Dara

Darby

Darci

Daria

Dasha

Dawn

Deanna

Deborah

Deedee

Delaney

Delle

Delphine

Demetria

Denise

Deonaid	**E (Girls)**	Eliora
Derry		Elizabeth
Deryn	Ealga	Ella
Desiree	Eanna	Eloise
Devany	Eartha	Elsa
Dextra	Ester	Emerald
Diala	Ebony	Emily
Diamond	Eca	Enid
Dielle	Edeline	Enrica
Dinah	Eden	Erianthe
Dionne	Ediah	Erin
Divine	Edrea	Ermine
Divonah	Edrice	Erna
Dolly	Effie	Eryl
Dolores	Eilah	Esme
Donna	Eileen	Estelle
Dorian	Eira	Etain
Drothy	Eirian	Eudora
Drina	Elaine	Eunice
Duena	Elle	Eva
Dulce	Eli	Evania
Dyvette	Elika	Evelyn

Everelda

Francoise

Freda

Ginny

Girisa

Giselle

Gleda

F (Girls)

Fabrizia

Faida

Faith

Faline

Farica

Farrah

Fatima

Fay

Feige

Felicia

Felora

Feodora

Fifi

Flia

Finola

Flo

Flora

Fontane

G (Girls)

Gabrielle

Gaia

Gail

Galena

Geela

Gelsey

Gen

Genea

Geona

Gerianne

Gertrude

Gia

Gialia

Gianina

Gigi

Gillian

Gina

Glenna

Gloria

Godiva

Grace

Grainne

Griselda

Guida

Gurice

Gwyneth

H (Girls)

Hadiya

Hadley

Haidee

Halia

Halina

Hania

Hannah

Hansine	Hope	Isla
Happy	Hosanna	Ismaela
Harmony	Hye	Italia
Harriet		Itiah
Harsha	**I (Girls)**	Iuana
Hateya	Ida	Ivory
Haven	Ilana	Ivria
Hayley	Ilehsa	Izusa
Hazel	Ilona	
Hediah	Ima	**J (Girls)**
Hedwig	Imara	Jacinta
Helen	Ina	Jacqueline
Helga	Indra	Jade
Helma	Ines	Jaira
Helmine	Ingrid	Jalila
Henrietta	Iola	Jamaica
Hera	Iona	Jamelia
Hesper	Irene	Jamila
Hilary	Irma	Janae
Hilda	Isabel	Jane
Holly	Isadora	Janet
Honey	Isaura	Janine

Jasmine	Joy	Kara
Jaya	Joyce	Karen
Jazlyn	Judith	Karida
Jean	Juliet	Karmel
Jelena	Jumana	Karissa
Jenelle		Karmen
Jennica	**K (Girls)**	Kasinda
Jennifer	Kaci	Kasmira
Jeralyn	Kaisa	Katherine
Jessica	Kaitlin	Katriel
Jesusa	Kalamela	Kawena
Jiana	Kalei	KaKeala
Jill	Kaligenia	Keara
Jirina	Kalilea	Keesha
Joan	Kalini	Kelly
Jocelyn	Kaliona	Kelsey
Jodelle	Kallolee	Kenda
Jolanta	Kamanika	Kendra
Jolie	Kamea	Kenisha
Jonella	Kamila	Kerry
Jonna	Kana	Kevina
Jorgina		Khalila

Kiara	Lady	Lavinia
Kiley	Laina	Lavonne
Kimberly	Laine	Leah
Kimimela	Lakea	Leala
Kira	Lala	Leanna
Kirsten	Lana	Lecia
Kishi	Lani	Leena
Kolenelia	Laniece	Lei
Kona	Lantha	Leigh
Korina	Lara	Leila
Kristen	Larena	Leilani
Kumi	Larine	Lena
Kuni	Larissa	Lenice
Kyla	Lashea	Leoda
Kyra	Lashell	Leona
Kyrie	Lashona	Leora
	Latasha	Leslie

L (Girls)

Lacey	Latifa	Letitia
Lachina	Latosha	Levia
Lacole	Latrice	Levina
Ladiva	Laura	Levona
	Laveda	Leana

Lida

Liesl

Lila

Lilac

Lilia

Lilith

Lilian

Lina

Linda

Lindsay

Linette

Linnea

Lisa

Lisandra

Litonya

Livona

Lola

Loni

Lorna

Lorraine

Lota

Love

Luca

Lucy

Lulu

Lura

Lydia

Lynn

M (Girls)

Mabel

Macy

Madia

Maecy

Maeiko

Maemi

Magena

Mahima

Mai

Maida

Maimi

Maiza

Maja

Malia

Malila

Malina

Malu

Manuela

Mara

Maraea

Maratina

Marcia

Marelda

Maretta

Margaret

Margaux

Marian

Marie

Marietta

Marilyn

Marina

Maris

Marni

Martha

Martina

Mary	Meredith	Mora
Masela	Meriel	Morela
Matilda	Merry	Moriah
Matrixa	Meryl	Myla
Maureen	Mia	Myra
Mavis	Michaela	Myrna
Maxine	Michelle	Myrtle
Maya	Mila	
Meara	Milcah	**N (Girls)**
Medea	Miliana	Nada
Meena	Milica	Nadia
Mehira	Mina	Nadira
Mela	Minda	Nadyah
Melanie	Minnie	Nahla
Melia	Miranda	Nami
Meliane	Mirella	Nana
Melissa	Miriam	Nancy
Melody	Missy	Naomi
Melvina	Miya	Narcissa
Mena	Moana	Narehsa
Mercedes	Mona	Natalie
Mercy	Monica	Nataniah

Natasha

Neda

Nehanda

Neola

Nera

Nerys

Nesiah

Nettie

Nicole

Nida

Nima

Nina

Nissa

Niva

Nizana

Noelan

Nola

Nona

Nora

Norell

Norna

Nova

Novella

Ninia

Nyla

Nyx

O (Girls)

Odelia

Odessa

Ohela

Ola

Oleda

Olga

Olina

Olisa

Olivia

Ona

Ondine

Onella

Onora

Oona

Ora

Orela

Oriana

Ornice

Orya

Otilie

Ozera

P (Girls)

Page

Paloma

Pamela

Pana

Pasha

Patricia

Paula

Pax

Paz

Pearl

Penelope

Peninah

Pheodora

Phoebe

Pilar

Pixie

Portia

Precious

Prima

Primrose

Princess

Purity

Q (Girls)

Queen

Quiana

Quintina

R (Girls)

Rachel

Radha

Rafaela

Rainbow

Ramona

Rana

Ranjanya

Ranya

Rasha

Rayna

Rea

Rebecca

Regina

Rehema

Renee

Rhoda

Rhonda

Ria

Riane

Rica

Rida

Rihana

Rima

Rinda

Rissa

Rita

Riva

Rochelle

Roma

Rosalind

Rosanna

Rose

Roselani

Rosemary

Roxanne

Ruby

Rufina

Runa

Ruth

S (Girls)

Sabina

Sachi

Sadira

Sakura

Salena

Salome

Salvia

Samantha

Samara

Samia

Samina	Shalanda	Sharon
Samira	Shalane	Shauna
Samuela	Shalyn	Shaunda
Sancia	Shameena	Shavonne
Sandra	Shamica	Shayleen
Sandyha	Shamira	Sheila
Sanya	Shana	Sheina
Sarah	Shanda	Shelley
Sasha	Shaneen	Sherice
Saura	Shaneika	Sherida
Savanna	Shanette	Sherika
Scarlett	Shanice	Shimona
Sela	Shanika	Shina
Selena	Shannon	Shirin
Seona	Shantaina	Shirley
Serena	Shantia	Shomera
Shaida	Shantrice	Shona
Shaina	Sharama	Sidonie
Shakeena	Sharanee	Sierra
Shakela	Sharlene	Sigrid
Shakira	Sharmaine	Silva
Shakonda		Silvia

Simone	Sydney	Tara
Sirena	Sylvia	Taree
Sissy	Syona	Tasha
Sitti		Tasmine
Sivanna	**T (Girls)**	Tate
Solona	Tabitha	Teleri
Soledad	Tacey	Terena
Sonia	Tahira	Teresa
Stacy	Taima	Tertia
Stellar	Takara	Tessa
Stephanie	Takeko	Tevy
Sugi	Taki	Thaleia
Sukey	Taki	Thea
Sula	Tala	Thekia
Sumi	Talisa	Thelma
Summer	Talitha	Theodora
Sundari	Talma	Theone
Sunniva	Tamara	Thin
Sunshine	Tamika	Tifanny
Suri	Tanaka	Tirtha
Susan	Tannishtha	Tirza
svea	Tanvi	Tish

Titania

Tomo

Tomiko

Tora

Tori

Toshala

Tracey

Tricia

Trixie

Tuesday

Tula

Tyra

Tzeira

Tzila

U (Girls)

Udele

Uinise

Ula

Ulrica

Umiko

Una

Urania

Urbana

Ursula

Ushi

V (Girls)

Vala

Valentia

Valerie

Valonia

Vana

Vanessa

Vanika

Varana

Varsha

Veda

Vedette

Veera

Vega

Velinda

Venus

Vera

Verena

Verity

Verna

Veronica

Vespera

Vesta

Vianna

Victoria

Vida

Vienna

Vilma

Vina

Viola

Violet

Virtue

Vita

Vivienne

W (Girls)

Wafa

Wakanda

Walda	Xenia	Yesenia
Wallis	Xin	Yeva
Wanda	Xuan	Yiehsa
Warda	Xylia	Yin
Welena		Yinji
Wendy	**Y (Girls)**	Yinina
Whitley	Yara	Yoki
Whitney	Yachi	Yoko
Wilda	Yacine	Yokohana
Wilfreda	Yaki	Yolanda
Wilma	Yakira	Yoluta
Winema	Yami	Yonina
Winona	Yamina	Yonni
Winter	Yamika	Yori
Wisdom	Yarina	Yosh
Wyetta	Yashill	Yosha
Wynelle	Yashilla	Yoshiko
Wynn-Wynn	Yasmine	Yoshino
	Yasu	Yovela
X (Girls)	Yelena	Yuki
Xandra	Yemina	Yula
Xaviera	Yepa	Yukiko

Yuriko

Yurika

Yusera

Yvette

Yvonne

Z (Girls)

Zada

Zafira

Zahira

Zahra

Zaira

Zakiya

Zalika

Zaneta

Zarifa

Zarina

Zarita

Zaza

Zea

Zeffa

Zehara

Zehira

Zel

Zelfa

Zelma

Zemira

Zemorah

Zen

Zenaida

Zenaima

Zenaira

Zenda

Zenobia

Zephyr

Zera

Zeraldina

Zesiro

Zetta

Zhane

Zho

Zhuo

Zia

Zimriah

Zina

Zinnia

Zippora

Ziram

Zita

Ziva

Zivanka

Zoe

Zoerela

Zoerena

Zola

Zona

Zora

Zorina

Zomina

Zulema

Zumi

Zuri

Zuwena

Zuzana

Zuzela

BABY NAMES FOR BOYS

A (Boys)

Adi

Aaron

Abel

Abiel

Ace

Acher

Achilles

Adam

Addison

Adler

Admon

Adolph

Adrian

Adriel

Aeson

Aki

Akihito

Ala

Alan

Albert

Alexander

Alfred

Allard

Altair

Alvis

Amadeus

Amadi

Amiel

Amir

Ammar

Amos

Amycus

Andor

Andrei

Andrew

Angelo

Anker

Ansel

Ark

Arvid

Auriel

Austin

Averill

Avidan

Axel

Az

Azarael

Azi

Aziel

B (Boys)

Bailey

Baldric

Baldwin

Ballard

Barak

Baram

Bardolf

Barlow	Bernard	Caelan
Barnes	Bert	Caesar
Baron	Berwyn	Caffar
Barry	Bill	Cain
Bartholomew	Birch	Caleb
Barton	Birkey	Calhoun
Baurice	Bishop	Cameron
Bayard	Bjorn	Camlo
Beal	Blaise	Cannon
Beanon	Blanford	Cappi
Beau	Boz	Carl
Bedford	Bob	Carlisle
Beldon	Bohdan	Carlos
Bello	Bojan	Carson
Benedict	Bond	Carter
Benjamin	Brandon	Carver
Bennett	Brigham	Casimir
Benson	Brody	Caspar
Bentley	Burton	Cassiel
Benzi		Cenon
Bergen	**C (Boys)**	Cerdic
Berkeley		Cerek

Chalfon

Chand

Chandler

Chaniel

Charles

Charlton

Chavin

Chester

Chetwin

Chico

Chilo

Chilton

Chip

Chitto

Christian

Christopher

Cid

Ciro

Clement

Cleon

Clifford

Clifton

Clinton

Clyde

Cody

Colby

D (Boys)

Dalbert

Dale

Dalfon

Dallas

Dalton

Dalziel

Damon

Dan

Daniel

Dante

Daren

Darius

Darnell

Darrick

Darwin

David

Dawson

Deacon

Dean

Deco

Delbert

Delewis

Delvin

Demond

Dempsey

Denley

Dennis

Dennison

Denver

Denzell

Derek

Deven

Devlin

Dewayne

Dewey

Digby

Dlynn

Dolan	Edison	Elroy
Donald	Edmund	Elton
Douglas	Edric	Elvio
Doyle	Edsel	Elvis
Drake	Edward	Emanuel
Drew	Edwin	Ember
Duane	Efron	Emerson
Dugan	Egan	Emile
Duncan	Egbert	Engelbert
Dunley	Egor	Enzo
Dunlop	Eilwyn	Eran
Dunmore	Einri	Eric
Duriel	Elan	Erland
	Elbert	Ernest
	Eldon	Erwin
	Eldridge	Esaias
E (Boys)	Eliran	Esau
Eamon	Ellard	Esmond
Earl	Elliot	Ethan
Eaton	Elman	Eugene
Eben	Elrad	Evan
Edan	Eldric	

F (Boys)

Fabian

Fabron

Fadi

Faisal

Farid

Faris

Farold

Faron

Farrell

Favian

Feilo

Felipe

Felix

Fergus

Feroz

Fidel

Filbert

Finn

Finnegan

Fitz

Fitzgerald

Fletcher

Flint

Floyd

Folant

Forbes

Ford

Forest

Fortune

Francis

Franklin

Franz

Fraser

Frederick

Freeman

Freemont

Frey

Frick

Fridolf

Fritz

Frodi

Frodo

Fulbert

Fuller

Fulton

Funsun

Fynn

G (Boys)

Gabriel

Gaetan

Gair

Gale

Galt

Galton

Galvin

Geronimo

Ghalib

Giannis

Gibson

Gifford

Gilbert

Gilby

Gilmore

Gino	**H (Boys)**	Hanford
Girvin		Hank
Galdwin	Hadi	Hanes
Glen	Hadley	Hannibal
Godfrey	Hadriel	Hanson
Godwin	Hadwin	Harbert
Goel	Hagan	Hardwin
Gomer	Hagley	Hardy
Granger	Haji	Harish
Grant	Hakan	Harley
Grantley	Haldor	Harold
Gray	Hale	Harper
Grayson	Hali	Harrington
Gregory	Halil	Harris
Griffin	Halim	Harry
Grover	Hallward	Hartford
Guilfford	Halsten	Hartley
Gus	Halton	Harvey
Gustaf	Hamilton	Hayden
Gustav	Hamish	Hector
Gustavo	Handel	Hedrick
Gyan		Hemene

Hercules

Herman

Hideo

Hilton

Hiroshi

Hoder

Hogan

Homer

Horton

Howin

Hudson

Humphrey

Hunt

Hunter

Huntley

Husayn

Husni

Hutton

Hyde

Hyo

Hyun

Hywel

I (Boys)

Ian

Ibrahim

Icarus

Ichiro

Ignatius

Ike

Ilias

Imrich

Inger

Ingram

Iram

Irvin

Irwing

Isaac

Isaiah

Ishaan

Isham

Ishaq

Isidore

Israel

Ivan

Ivor

J (Boys)

Jabez

Jabir

Jacinto

Jack

Jackson

Jacob

Jadon

Jaden

Jafar

Jafari

Jairus

Jamal

Jamar

James

Jameson

Janson

Janus

Japeth	Joseph	Kareem
Jareb	Josh	Kasim
Jareth	Joshua	Keaton
Jaron	Josiah	Kebb
Jarvis	Jude	Keefe
Jason	Julian	Keenan
Jasper	Julius	Keiji
Javas	Jun	Keith
Javier	Junior	Kelby
Javon	Juri	Kell
Jean	Justine	Kelton
Jedrek		Kendrik
Jefferson	**K (Boys)**	Kenley
Jeffrey	Kadmiel	Kenn
Jeremy	Kaemon	Kennedy
Jericho	Kahil	Kenneth
Jerrell	Kaiser	Kent
Jesse	Kale	Kenton
Jethro	Kaleo	Kenward
Jett	Kalil	Kenway
Jordan	Kaniel	Kenyon
Jorge		Keoki

Keon	Koi	Langley
Keoni	Kornel	Langston
Kermitt	Kort	Larkin
Kerry	Kuper	Laron
Kersen	Kyan	Larry
Kerwin	Kyle	Lasairian
Keshon		Lawford
Kester	**L (Boys)**	Lawrence
Kevin	La Roy	Lawson
Kidd	La Vonn	Lazarus
Kieran	Ladd	Lee
Kiho	Lael	Leighton
Killian	Lake	Lemuel
King	Lamar	Lennon
Kingsley	Lambert	Lennor
Kingston	Lamonte	Lennox
Kipp	Lancelot	Leo
Kirby	Lander	Leon
Klemens	Landon	Leonard
Klement	Langdon	Leopold
Knight	Langford	Leroy
Knowx		Lester

Levi

Lewin

Lex

Leyland

Liem

Lindberg

Lindell

Linford

Linton

Lionel

Llewelyn

Lloyd

Logan

Loki

Lon

Long

Lord

Louis

Lovell

Lucan

Lucas

Ludwig

Luister

Lyle

M (Boys)

Mac

Mac Adam

Macalister

Macbride

Maccoy

Macdonald

Macdougal

Mackenzie

Macmahon

Madison

Maguire

Mahir

Mahon

Major

Makarios

Makimo

Malachi

Malcolm

Malik

Mallory

Maloney

Malvern

Manachu

Manco

Mander

Manley

Mansur

Manu

Marcus

Marden

Mario

Marion

Marley

Marlow

Marsh

Mart

Martin

Marvin

Mason

Mattheo

Matthew

Maurice

Maxwell

Mayer

Medwin

Melvin

Merlin

N (Boys)

Natal

Nathan

Navin

Neil

Nelson

Nemo

Neper

Neptune

Nero

Nesbit

Nestor

Neto

Neville

Nevin

Newell

Newman

Newton

Niaz

Nicabar

Nicholas

Nicodemus

Nien

Nigan

Nigel

Nikolai

Nikolao

Nikomedes

Nimrod

Nipton

Niram

Nisan

Nishad

Nixon

Nizar

Noah

Noam

Nodin

Noe

Noel

Noor

Norbert

Norman

Norris

Norton

Norvell

Norvin

Norward

Norwood

Noy

Nyoy

Numa

Nuncio

Nuren

Nuri

Nusair

O (Boys)

Oakley	Oleg	Orville
Oba	Olery	Orvin
Obadiah	Oliver	Osbert
Oberon	Olney	Osborn
Obet	Olorun	Oscar
Obi	Olujimi	Osman
Obike	Omanand	Osmond
Octavius	Omar	Osred
Odell	Omri	Osric
Odion	Onan	Osten
Odolf	Onani	Oswald
Odysseus	Ondrei	Oswen
Ogden	Oran	Oswin
Ogun	Oren	Othman
Oisin	Orford	Othniel
Oistin	Orion	Otis
Ojore	Orlando	Otto
Oko	Oro	Oved
Okon	Oron	Owen
Ola	Orrick	Oyo
Olaf	Orson	Oxford
Oldrich	Orton	Oz

Ozni

P (Boys)

Paco

Paddy

Pagiel

Pal

Palmer

Pancho

Parker

Parlan

Paxton

Parnell

Parr

Parry

Pascal

Patrick

Pattin

Patton

Patwin

Paul

Paxton

Pearson

Pelagios

Penley

Penn

Pepin

Percival

Percy

Perry

Peter

Peyton

Phelps

Philip

Philo

Phio

Phoenix

Phthisis

Pias

Piercy

Pillan

Pin

Pino

Pio

Piro

Pitney

Pitt

Placido

Plato

Pollard

Pollux

Pomeroy

Ponce

Pontus

Porter

Powell

Pravin

Prem

Prescott

Presley

Preston

Primo

Prince

Prosper

Pryor

Purvis

Putnam

Q (Boys)

Qued

Quennell

Quintin

Qilliam

Quincy

Quinn

Quinto

Quirin

R (Boys)

Rabi

Radcliff

Radford

Radley

Radnor

Radwan

Rafa

Rafi

Ragner

Rahman

Raiden

Rajab

Ralph

Ram

Ramsay

Rance

Randolph

Ranen

Ragner

Ranson

Raoul

Raphael

Rashid

Rav

Ravi

Ray

Rayburn

Raymond

Read

Redley

Redman

Redmond

Redford

Regan

Reginald

Remus

Renny

Renton

Renzo

Reuben

Reuel

Rex

Reynard

Reynold

Rez

Richard

Richmond

Rider

Rigley

Riley

Rimon	Rothwell	Safa
Ringo	Rover	Sahil
Ripley	Rowell	Said
Rishon	Roy	Samson
Risley	Royce	Samuel
Robert	Rozen	Sancho
Robertson	Rudd	Sanford
Robinson	Rufus	Sanjay
Rocco	Rumford	Santiago
Rock	Rune	Santosh
Rockley	Rupert	Saul
Roderick	Ruppy	Saville
Rodman	Ruskin	Sawyer
Rodney	Ruswell	Saxon
Rohin	Rutley	Scott
Roman	Ryan	Seabert
Romeo	Rye	Sean
Ronald		Seanan
Ronel	**S (Boys)**	Seaton
Rooney	Sachiel	Sebastian
Rosh	Sadler	Sef
Ross		Selby

Selwyn	Sigurd	Stafford
Serge	Sigwald	Stamos
Sett	Simon	Stancie
Severin	Simpson	Stancliff
Severino	Sinjon	Stanfield
Seward	Siphon	Stanford
Seymour	Siva	Stanley
Shafar	Slade	Stanmore
Shakil	Slavin	Stanton
Shamir	Sloan	Stanway
Shank	Smedley	Stanwick
Snaley	Smith	Stanwood
Shawnel	Socrates	Stavross
Shelby	Sofian	Stein
Shen	Solomon	Steinar
Sherman	sonny	Stephen
Shiloh	Soren	Sterne
Shiva	Sorley	Stewart
Shomer	Sorrell	Stewart
Sidwell	Sovann	Stockley
Sigfrid	Spear	Stoddard
Sigmund	Spencer	Storm

Stratford	Talman	Theo
Sture	Tan	Theron
Sudi	Tank	Thomas
Sujay	Tanner	Thor
Sujit	Tanni	Thorbert
Sullivan	Tano	Thorley
Sully	Tarik	Thorton
Sumantra	Tate	Tibor
Sunil	Tavis	Tilden
Sutcliff	Tavor	Till
Sven	Taylor	Tito
Sveinn	Tennesee	Titus
Swinford	Tennyson	Toab
Swinto	Terence	Tobias
Sylvester	Teryl	Tobbar
	Tevin	Todd

T (Boys)

	Thane	Tomer
Tad	Thang	Tomi
Tahoma	Thanos	Tony
Taj	Thatcher	Tord
Tal	Theodore	Torrell
Talli		Torin

Torrance	Ulric	Van
Travis	Ulysses	Vance
Trayton	Umar	Vandyke
Tristan	Umed	Varden
Tuan	Uner	Varen
Tudor	Urien	Varick
Tuong	Ursan	Vasil
Turner	Urvil	Vaughn
Twyford	Ustin	Vencel
Ty	Uthman	Verdun
Tydeus	Uttam	Verlin
Tyke	Uziah	Verrill
Tyler	Uziel	Victor
Tymon		Vidor
Tyrone	**V (Boys)**	Vijay
	Vail	Viliami
U (Boys)	Valdemar	Vilio
Udolf	Valdemore	vilmos
Ugo	Valentin	Vincent
Ulf	Valentine	Vino
Ulmer	Valin	Virgil
		Vitalis

Vito

Vitus

Vladlen

Vladimir

Volker

Von

Vui

W (Boys)

Wade

Wadley

Wagner

Wail

Wakefield

Wakeley

Walden

Waldo

Walker

Wallace

Walter

Walker

Wallace

Walter

Walton

Wardell

Wadley

Warren

Wayne

Webber

Webley

Welborne

Welby

Weldon

Welford

Wellington

Wendell

Wentworth

Werner

Wesley

Westcott

Wharton

Whitby

Whitfield

Whitford

Wilbur

Wilford

Wilfred

Wilkinson

William

Williamson

Wilmer

Wilson

Wilton

Windsor

Winfield

Winslow

Wolfe

Woodfield

Woodford

Woodville

Worth

Wright

Wybert

X (Boys)

Xanthus

Xavier

Xenon

Xerxes

Ximen

Xylon

Y (Boys)

Yadin

Yair

Yancy

Yannis

Yardley

Yarin

Yash

Yasin

Yeriel

Ymir

Yong

York

Yosef

Yoshi

Yuan

Yucel

Yul

Yurich

Yuri

Yusuf

Yves

Z (Boys)

Zaccheus

Zachariah

Zafar

Zahid

Zim

Zaki

Zamiel

Zamir

Zared

Zarek

Zayn

Zdeslav

Ze'ev

Zeheb

Zeke

Zend

Zephyrus

Zethus

Zeus

Zevadiah

Zevid

Zhu

Zhuang

Zimraan

Zimri

Zindan

Zindel

Zion

Zitomer

Ziv

Zivah

Ziveh

Ziyad

Zoltin

Zomeir

Zow

Zubiri

Zuriel

Zwi

Zygmunt

Zygy

Zygg

UNISEX BABY NAMES

A (Unisex)

Ade

Andi

Afa

Afi

Agathias

Aineas

Ailesh

Ainmire

Aisea

Ake

Aviah

Ax

B (Unisex)

Baden

Bal

Balin

Barra

Bay

Beattie

Beilish

Bem

Benes

Ber

Berg

Berry

Bevan

Bevis

Bing

Binh

Bliss

Borg

Boyce

Boyne

Brent

Brett

Bry

Bryd

C (Unisex)

Cadi

Cai

Caley

Camden

Camey

Can

Canice

Carmine

Carr

Case

Chai

Chal

Cham

Chan

Chane

Chang

Chanti

Chau	Dema	Dubh
Chauncey	Denby	Duff
Che	Dennel	Dumin
Chi	Deniz	Dun
Cory	Denzil	Dyer
Con	Deron	Dyre
	Deror	

D (Unisex)

Dada	Deshi	
Dag	Destin	**E (Unisex)**
Dai	Dewi	Eallair
Daire	Dezydery	Edel
Dakota	Didier	Einar
Daly	Dilip	Eliaz
Dane	Dinh	Elmore
Dang	Dirk	Elen
Danior	Dives	Eloy
Dar	Diya	Ettore
Darcy	Dob	Eunan
Daudi	Dooley	Euston
Dax	Dor	Evander
Delmar	Dreng	Evzen
		Ezra

F (Unisex)

Fabrice

Fadey

Fagan

Fairleigh

Falak

Fale

Fane

Farr

Fathi

Fergal

Fiachra

Fife

Finan

Finian

Frayne

Freedom

G (Unisex)

Gage

Galen

Gamba

Gan

Garai

Garek

Garner

Garth

Gary

Geary

Gene

Genty

Gerlach

Germaine

Gervase

Gethin

Gig

Glaisne

Glyn

Gore

Gulshan

Griffith

Guy

Gyasi

Gylfi

H (Unisex)

Hajj

Hala

Halley

Ham

Hamal

Hamlet

Hastin

Hau

Hayes

Heaven

Heber

Heneli

Henley

Henning

Herleif

Hermes

Hevel

Hewney

Hien	Ifor	Jabin
Hilel	Ihsan	Jachym
Hinun	Ikaia	Jacy
Hirsh	Ikale	Jaegar
Hoa	Ilom	Jael
Hoc	Ilya	Jahan
Hod	Ingvar	Jaja
Hodding	Inigo	Jal
Hoku	Inico	Jalen
Hola	Innes	Jan
Holic	Inoke	Jarah
Horst	Ion	Jasha
Hosea	Ira	Jaspal
Howe	Isas	Java
Howie	Isha	Javan
Hoyt	Isikeli	Jay
Hu	Ismah	Jed
Huxley	Iye	Jehan
		Jela

I (Unisex)

J (Unisex)

Jenkin

Idi	Jaan	Jensi
Idris		Jerbie

73

Jernie

Jex

Jibri

Jie

Johar

Joeff

Joji

Jojo

Jomei

Joza

K (Unisex)

Kal

Kaleu

Kanu

Kass

Kaul

Kielli

Keoia

Kesse

Kimo

Kin

Kincaid

Kwintyn

Kyros

L (Unisex)

Laird

Lais

Lallo

Lane

Lanty

Lap

Lars

Lateef

Lithium

Latimer

Lavi

Le sonn

Leibel

Leith

Leor

Li

Like

Linus

Leron

Lynch

M (Unisex)

Maalin

Machir

Mafi

Magee

Malo

Mandel

Mansel

Marville

Mabar

Marek

Marwan

Meir

Mikasi

Mohe

Moran

Moray

Mori

Morley

Morse

Mosi

Muir

Munchkin

Murphy

Myers

N (Unisex)

Nahele

Naim

Nam

Nard

Nav

Naveed

Niutei

Nuru

O (Unisex)

Odissan

Ondrej

P (Unisex)

Paze

Penne

Pericles

Q (Unisex)

Quinn

Quincy

Quentin

Quince

Quarry

R (Unisex)

Rabbie

Rad

Red

Raider

Raini

Ran

Renen

Reece

Reeve

Rei

Rene

Resheph

Rhan

Ridge

Rio

Roe

Roni

Rory

S (Unisex)

Sabin

Sabir

Sagar

Sahn

Saula

Sauts

Semi	Tau	Vachel
Sen	Tava	Valmiki
Seoirse	Tawl	Vane
September	Temple	Vanya
Sese	Thiassi	Vardhamma
Shalom	Tho	Varun
Sharef	Thou	Vasu
Sholto	Thuc	Veai
Siencyn	Tien	Veasna
Simidh	Toril	Veere
Sinclair	Trent	Viet
Starr	Trey	Vihs
Stig		Vinay
Styles		Vladle
Syon		Vlas

U (Unisex)

Ull

Uri

T (Unisex)

Urian

W (Unisex)

Tab	Useni	Waban
Tabbai	Usi	Wabaunsee
Taheton	Usie	Waedie
Tami		Wanhattan

V (Unisex)

Wajih	Weshie	Winthrop
Wakeman	Wetherby	Wisia
Wakiza	Whalley	Wisse
Walaka	Whistler	Wit
Walcott	Whitcomb	Wolcott
Walwyn	White	Won shik
Wanjohi	Whitelaw	Wuyi
Wapi	Whiteford	Wynono
Warburton	Whitlock	
Ware	Whitmore	**X (Unisex)**
Waree	Whoopi	Xini
Warefare	Wicahpi	Xino
Warefore	Wichado	Xuantan
Washburn	Widad	Xylian
Wattan	Wilanu	Xyxylian
Waverly	Willeey	
Waverlyn	Willoughby	**Y (Unisex)**
Wei	Willow	Yaa
Wells	Wilny	Yaara
Wen	Wingate	Yachine
Wenilo	Winnemucca	Yael
Wendice		Yaffa

77

Yalika	Yuluviz	Zubay
Yamkan		Zucay
Yardenan	**Z (Unisex)**	Zuleika
Yarmil	Zaa	Zuwein
Yasu	Zada	Zuwi
Yasui	Zadan	
Yejade	Zahren	
Yeminne	Zahrev	
Yetti	Zan	
Yieve	Zin	
Yieva	Zind	
Yinn	Zint	
Yoi	Ziono	
Yoiri	Zionor	
Yoirij	Ziracuny	
Yornj	Zlata	
Yorijo	Zlate	
Yorijan	Zocha	
Yorijean	Zooch	
Yormijin	Zoherert	
Yulu	Zontz	
Yuluver		

BONUS

BABY NAMING WORKSHEETS

How should you use these worksheets? Like the rest of this book, take or leave whatever you like from the following worksheets. All are meant to be helpful, but if some don't seem to speak to you particularly, feel free to skip them if you so choose.

LET'S BRAINSTORM, BABY

Baby Naming Worksheet No. 1

In this worksheet, feel free to write all over it, scribble, doodle, whatever you feel! We have some suggestions to get the brain juices flowing, but ignore our questions and make up your own if you like!

1. Name 10 names. Right now! Any 10 names.

2. Name your favorite movie characters.

3. Name your favorite book characters.

4. Choose 5 obscure names from your family tree. Go!

5. What is your favorite flower?

6. What is your favorite season?

7. What day of the week is it?

8. What is your favorite weather?

9. Write down 2 names that you like. Now combine them into 1.

10. Write down the name of someone you admire.

11. Open up your Google Maps. Close your eyes and move your mouse around. Open your eyes. What's the nearest town name or landmark?

12. Write down 10 names you don't like. Now think: What if this were your best friend's name?

13. Write down your favorite letter. Write down 10 words that start with this letter.

14. Write down your three favorite pet names.

15. Write a name that sounds strong.

16. Write a name that sounds beautiful.

17. Write a name that sounds like a good friend.

18. Write a name that sounds like a leader.

19. Write a name that sounds like a person who can make you laugh.

20. Make up a name you've never heard of before.

FINDING YOUR VALUES

Baby Naming Worksheet No. 2

In this worksheet, you'll reflect on what's important to you in a name. There are no right answers; be honest with yourself, and true to yourself, to make sure you are choosing a name for your future child for the right reasons. There are two sections here, so you and your partner can both fill it out:

PARTNER 1

When naming my child, I most care about pleasing (choose as many as apply):

☐ Myself ☐ My partner ☐ My child about to be born ☐ My other children ☐ My father v My mother ☐ My mother-in-law ☐ My father-in-law ☐ My grandparents ☐ My husband's grandparents ☐ My siblings ☐ My partner's siblings ☐ Other relatives of mine ☐ Other relatives' of my partners ☐ My friends ☐ My partner's friends ☐ The community I live in with my partner ☐ Friends on social media ☐ Strangers I will meet with my child
☐ Other:

Now you can only choose ONE of the above. Which do you choose?

How will this affect your naming choice? *(i.e., I will choose a name that honors my maternal grandmother. I will choose a name that sounds professional for my child's future.)*

When naming my child, I value (choose as many as apply):

☐ Tradition ☐ Fitting in ☐ Being unique ☐ Honoring family ☐ Culture ☐ Alliteration ☐ Meaning & Origin ☐ Other:

Now you can only choose ONE of the above. Which do you choose?

How will this affect your naming choice? *(i.e., I will find a names that feels special and unique, or I will research the meaning of my top name choices)*

PARTNER 2

When naming my child, I most care about pleasing (choose as many as apply):

☐ Myself ☐ My partner ☐ My child about to be born ☐ My other children ☐ My father v My mother ☐ My mother-in-law ☐ My father-in-law ☐ My grandparents ☐ My husband's grandparents ☐ My siblings ☐ My partner's siblings ☐ Other relatives of mine ☐ Other relatives' of my partners ☐ My friends ☐ My partner's friends ☐ The community I live in with my partner ☐ Friends on social media ☐ Strangers I will meet with my child
☐ Other:

Now you can only choose ONE of the above. Which do you choose?

How will this affect your naming choice? *(i.e., I will choose a name that honors my maternal grandmother. I will choose a name that sounds professional for my child's future.)*

When naming my child, I value (choose as many as apply):

☐ Tradition ☐ Fitting in ☐ Being unique ☐ Honoring family ☐ Culture ☐ Alliteration ☐ Meaning & Origin ☐ Other:

Now you can only choose ONE of the above. Which do you choose?

How will this affect your naming choice? *(i.e., I will find a names that feels special and unique, or I will research the meaning of my top name choices)*

YOUR BABY NAME TOP 10 LIST

Baby Naming Worksheet No. 3

Use this worksheet when you have narrowed down your names to a few top contenders. With the help of this worksheet, you will evaluate each name based on some important factors I have written about in my book.

Feel free to split five and five names with your partner, or copy/print extra sheets so you can both fill out as many as you like.

1. Name:

I have considered/checked: ☐ First name with last name ☐ First name with middle name ☐ First name with middle & last ☐ Initials ☐ Nicknames ☐ Rhyming nicknames ☐ Pop culture associations ☐ Popularity over time/history of name ☐ This name fits a young adult/middle-aged person as well as a baby/child

I like this name because:

I am hesitant about this name because:

This name reminds me of:

How does my partner feel about this name? ☐ Loves it ☐ Likes it but not totally convinced ☐   Doesn't like it that much ☐ Does not like it at all

Additional Notes:

2. Name:

I have considered/checked:

☐ First name with last name ☐ First name with middle name ☐ First name with middle & last ☐ Initials ☐ Nicknames ☐ Rhyming nicknames ☐ Pop culture associations ☐ Popularity over time/history of name ☐ This name fits a young adult/middle-aged person as well as a baby/child

I like this name because:

I am hesitant about this name because:

This name reminds me of:

How does my partner feel about this name? ☐ Loves it ☐ Likes it but not totally convinced ☐ Doesn't like it that much ☐ Does not like it at all

Additional Notes:

3. Name:

I have considered/checked:

☐ First name with last name ☐ First name with middle name ☐ First name with middle & last ☐ Initials ☐ Nicknames ☐ Rhyming nicknames ☐ Pop culture associations ☐ Popularity over time/history of name ☐ This name fits a young adult/middle-aged person as well as a baby/child

I like this name because:

I am hesitant about this name because:

This name reminds me of:

How does my partner feel about this name? ☐ Loves it ☐ Likes it but not totally convinced ☐   Doesn't like it that much ☐ Does not like it at all

Additional Notes:

4. Name:

I have considered/checked:

☐ First name with last name ☐ First name with middle name ☐ First name with middle & last ☐ Initials ☐ Nicknames ☐ Rhyming nicknames ☐ Pop culture associations ☐ Popularity over time/history of name ☐ This name fits a young adult/middle-aged person as well as a baby/child

I like this name because:

I am hesitant about this name because:

This name reminds me of:

How does my partner feel about this name? ☐ Loves it ☐ Likes it but not totally convinced ☐ Doesn't like it that much ☐ Does not like it at all

Additional Notes:

5. Name:

I have considered/checked:

☐ First name with last name ☐ First name with middle name ☐ First name with middle & last ☐ Initials ☐ Nicknames ☐ Rhyming nicknames ☐ Pop culture associations ☐ Popularity over time/history of name ☐ This name fits a young adult/middle-aged person as well as a baby/child

I like this name because:

I am hesitant about this name because:

This name reminds me of:

How does my partner feel about this name? ☐ Loves it ☐ Likes it but not totally convinced ☐ Doesn't like it that much ☐ Does not like it at all

Additional Notes:

6. Name:

I have considered/checked:

☐ First name with last name ☐ First name with middle name ☐ First name with middle & last ☐ Initials ☐ Nicknames ☐ Rhyming nicknames ☐ Pop culture associations ☐ Popularity over time/history of name ☐ This name fits a young adult/middle-aged person as well as a baby/child

I like this name because:

I am hesitant about this name because:

This name reminds me of:

How does my partner feel about this name? ☐ Loves it ☐ Likes it but not totally convinced ☐ Doesn't like it that much ☐ Does not like it at all

Additional Notes:

7. Name:

I have considered/checked:

☐ First name with last name ☐ First name with middle name ☐ First name with middle & last ☐ Initials ☐ Nicknames ☐ Rhyming nicknames ☐ Pop culture associations ☐ Popularity over time/history of name ☐ This name fits a young adult/middle-aged person as well as a baby/child

I like this name because:

I am hesitant about this name because:

This name reminds me of:

How does my partner feel about this name? ☐ Loves it ☐ Likes it but not totally convinced ☐ Doesn't like it that much ☐ Does not like it at all

Additional Notes:

8. Name:

I have considered/checked:

☐ First name with last name ☐ First name with middle name ☐ First name with middle & last ☐ Initials ☐ Nicknames ☐ Rhyming nicknames ☐ Pop culture associations ☐ Popularity over time/history of name ☐ This name fits a young adult/middle-aged person as well as a baby/child

I like this name because:

I am hesitant about this name because:

This name reminds me of:

How does my partner feel about this name? ☐ Loves it ☐ Likes it but not totally convinced ☐ Doesn't like it that much ☐ Does not like it at all

Additional Notes:

9. Name:

I have considered/checked:

☐ First name with last name ☐ First name with middle name ☐ First name with middle & last ☐ Initials ☐ Nicknames ☐ Rhyming nicknames ☐ Pop culture associations ☐ Popularity over time/history of name ☐ This name fits a young adult/middle-aged person as well as a baby/child

I like this name because:

I am hesitant about this name because:

This name reminds me of:

How does my partner feel about this name? ☐ Loves it ☐ Likes it but not totally convinced ☐ Doesn't like it that much ☐ Does not like it at all

Additional Notes:

10. Name:

I have considered/checked:

☐ First name with last name ☐ First name with middle name ☐ First name

with middle & last ☐ Initials ☐ Nicknames ☐ Rhyming nicknames ☐ Pop

culture associations ☐ Popularity over time/history of name ☐ This name fits

a young adult/middle-aged person as well as a baby/child

I like this name because:

I am hesitant about this name because:

This name reminds me of:

How does my partner feel about this name? ☐ Loves it ☐ Likes it but not

totally convinced ☐   Doesn't like it that much ☐ Does not like it at all

Additional Notes:

FURTHER READING & THANK YOU

We like to get real reader feedback, and would love to hear if you enjoyed the book, found it useful, or have suggestions for improvement. Please leave us a review on Amazon.

Entering this link into your browser will take you right to your reviews page: bit.ly/babynamesreview

Looking for more names?

The sequel to this guide, "!0,000 Baby Names List," is now available in the Amzon store in both paperback and ebook.

You can buy it at: bitly.com/10kbabynames

And you're invited to subscribe to our Free Book Club at **www.walnutpub.com** to receive more books from author Aston Sanderson, and free new releases from Walnut Publishing.

19664367R00063

Printed in Poland
by Amazon Fulfillment
Poland Sp. z o.o., Wrocław